Gardening Guides

Creative Gardening

GROWING PLANTS UPSIDE DOWN, IN WATER, AND MORE

by Lisa J. Amstutz

CAPSTONE PRESS
a capstone imprint

Snap Books are published by Capstone Press,
1710 Roe Crest Drive, North Mankato, Minnesota 56003
www.mycapstone.com

Library of Congress Cataloging-in-Publication Data
Names: Amstutz, Lisa J., author.
Title: Creative gardening : growing plants upside down, in water, and more /
   Lisa Amstutz.
Description: North Mankato, Minnesota : Capstone Press, [2016] | Series: Snap
   books. Gardening guides | Audience: Ages 8-14._ | Audience: Grades 4 to
   6._ | Includes bibliographical references and index.
Identifiers: LCCN 2015031200|
ISBN 978-1-4914-8237-7 (library binding) |
ISBN 978-1-4914-8627-6 (eBook PDF)
Subjects: LCSH: Gardening for children—Juvenile literature. | Container
   gardening—Juvenile literature. | Gardening to attract wildlife—Juvenile
   literature.
Classification: LCC SB457 .A47 2016 | DDC 635.9—dc23
LC record available at http://lccn.loc.gov/2015031200

Editorial Credits
Abby Colich, editor; Bobbie Nuytten and Tracy McCabe; designers;
Morgan Walters and Tracy Cummins, media researchers;
Laura Manthe, production specialist

Image Credits
All photographs by Capstone Studio: Karon Dubke with the exception of:
Shutterstock: Africa Studio, 19, AN NGUYEN, 7 Middle, AnjelikaGr, 5, 18,
Antonova Anna, Back Cover, inh Thanh Bui, 21 Left, Lucy Baldwin, Back
Cover, 15, MiVa, 7 Left, Nella, 7 Right, Richard Griffin, 11 Bottom, Sarunyu_
foto, 27, unpict, Back Cover, 11 Top, wong yu liang, 30, Yasonya, 4, Yellowj, 31
Design Elements by Shutterstock

Printed in the United States of America.
009710R

Table of Contents

Get Growing

What better way to express your creativity than with a garden? Grow plants that you can use to create your own dye, and then make your own tie-dye T-shirt. Create a hanging garden or flowery footwear. Use your imagination to come up with even more creative gardens of your own.

Plants need a few basic things to grow: sunshine, water, and good soil. If you're planting an outdoor garden, choose your site carefully. Make sure it gets plenty of light throughout the day. Place indoor plants near a sunny window, and be sure to water them regularly. Water plants every few days or whenever the soil starts to feel dry. Make sure there are holes on the bottom of your container so water can drain.

Before you start, you'll need to gather a few tools and supplies. Potting soil is a must for container plants. Soil from your garden or yard will not allow water to drain properly. A trowel comes in handy for scooping soil and digging holes. You'll also need a spray bottle or watering can to water container plants.

Pick a spot, gather your supplies, and get growing!

FEEDING YOUR CONTAINER PLANTS

Feed your houseplants regularly during the growing season. Add liquid fertilizer to the water in your spray bottle, or push fertilizer spikes into the soil. Be sure to follow the instructions on the package.

Japanese String Garden

These beautiful hanging balls are an ancient Japanese art called *kokedama*. They are so much fun, you won't want to make just one!

What You'll Need

- 3.5 cups (790 grams) peat soil
- 1.5 cups (340 grams) *akadama* (bonsai soil)
- 1 asparagus fern
- 1 square foot (30 square centimeters) sheet moss
- 4 yards (3.7 meters) colorful cotton string
- large metal pan
- water
- hook or place to hang your plant

Instructions

1. Soak sheet moss in a pan of water for an hour before using.

2. Mix peat soil and *akadama*. Sprinkle water over the mixture until it feels damp and sticks together when you squeeze it.

3. Remove fern carefully from its pot. Brush off the soil from around its roots.

4. Pack soil mix around the roots to form a ball about the size of a grapefruit.

5. Place your ball in the center of the sheet moss. Wrap the sheet moss around it.

6. Start wrapping string around the ball to hold the moss firmly in place. Wrap about 10 times, in all different directions.

7. Tie off the end of the string on one of the strands around the ball. Cut off the extra string.

8. Tie the cut piece of string to a strand near the top of the ball. Cut it to whatever height you like. Have an adult help you hang it from a hook.

9. Water your *kokedama* whenever the ball begins to feel light and the soil seems dry. Dunk it in a bucket of water until bubbles stop coming to the top, about 5 to 10 minutes. Lift it out, and squeeze gently. Let it drain before rehanging.

MORE PLANT CHOICES

Try hanging other plants such as philodendrons, orchids, begonias, coleus, staghorn ferns, echeverias, and other succulents. You can use different colors of string as well.

Happy Little Hedgehog

Reuse old water bottles to make this cheery little hedgehog planter. You can also use different sizes of bottles to create a whole hedgehog family!

What You'll Need

- scissors
- plastic water bottle
- twine
- craft glue
- 2 buttons
- black paint and paintbrush (if bottle cap is not already black)
- potting soil
- ornamental grass seed

Instructions

1. Have an adult help you cut a large rectangle out of one side of the bottle with scissors.

2. Spread glue over the bottle. Wrap twine around, covering the whole bottle. Cut twine as you get to the cut out rectangle, and start again on the other side so that the rectangle remains open. Trim off any extra twine.

3. Glue buttons onto the top of the bottle for eyes.

4. If cap isn't already black, paint and let dry.

5. Put potting soil into the rectangle until the bottle is full.

6. Sprinkle grass seed over the soil. Set it in a sunny place.

7. Water your hedgehog daily if you keep it outdoors. If it is indoors, water two to three times a week, or as needed to keep the soil moist.

MORE ANIMALS

What other animals can you make with a water bottle? Use your imagination!

"Just for Kicks" Garden

Fancy or not, old footwear makes a fun planter. Tuck a begonia into a boot, or stick a snapdragon in your sneaker. Let your imagination "run" wild! Plant several shoes to create a whole garden.

What You'll Need

- old shoe or boot
- nail, awl, or drill
- potting soil
- hen and chicks plants or other small succulents

Instructions

1. Have an adult make several holes in the sole of the boot or shoe. This will allow water to drain out. If the sole is soft, use a nail or awl to poke holes. If it is hard leather, drill holes.

2. Fill the shoe with potting soil.

3. Plant the hen and chicks, pressing soil firmly around them to hold them in place.

4. Water the soil well.

5. Set your shoe planter in a sunny place. Water as needed. If you keep it indoors, place a tray under it to catch the water as it drains.

MORE SHOE GARDENS

Buy old shoes from a thrift store if you don't have any at home. Plant several, and display them on a railing, set them on the steps of a ladder, or hang them from a wall. Try planting annual flowers such as impatiens, pansies, and begonias in your shoe garden.

Creative Container Garden

What's even better than recycling? Upcycling! Give old objects a new life by turning them into creative planters. Start with this clementine box. You can use the chalkboard surface to write yourself a reminder to water your plants, or share another message. Then see what else you can upcycle.

What You'll Need

- wooden clementine box
- sandpaper
- chalkboard paint
- paintbrush
- drill
- foil or plastic
- pencil
- potting soil
- 3 pansy and 3 petunia plants
- chalk

Instructions

1. Remove any stickers from the clementine box.
2. Rub the box with sandpaper to remove any rough areas or sharp edges.
3. Paint the sides of the box with chalkboard paint. Let it dry for several hours.
4. Add a second coat of paint. Let it dry overnight.
5. Have an adult drill five drainage holes in the bottom of the box—one near each corner and one in the center.
6. Line the inside of the box with plastic or foil. Poke holes in it with a pencil to line up with the holes in the base of the box.
7. Fill box half full of potting soil. Set the plants inside. Fill in potting soil around them, and press firmly to hold them in place. Leave 1 inch (2.5 cm) of space at the top.
8. Using a clean spray bottle, mist plants daily to keep the soil moist.

UPCYCLED PLANTERS

What else could you turn into a planter? Look for unused items around your home and garage. The possibilities are endless. Remember to ask for permission before you use something from your house. You may also need an adult to help you drill drainage holes in your upcycled planter.

- *Plant a row of flowers or lettuce in a section of gutter. Attach it to a porch or deck railing.*
- *Plant flowers in an old dresser drawer or basket.*
- *Check your kitchen cupboards for old pots, colanders, or plastic containers to turn into planters.*

Ivy in a Jar

Did you know some plants can grow without any soil at all? Put some ivy in a jar of water, and watch its roots go wild. Use craft supplies such as paint or ribbon to dress up your jar, or display in your own creative way.

What You'll Need

- clear glass jar with a wide base
- aquarium gravel
- cutting of ivy or another plant from the list below
- liquid fertilizer
- rainwater or distilled water

Instructions

1. Take a cutting of ivy or another plant. To take a cutting, clip off a piece of the plant just below a leaf.

2. Place the roots or cut edge of the plant at the bottom of the jar. Add 1 to 2 inches (2.5 to 5 cm) of aquarium gravel to hold it in place.

3. Slowly add water. Do not cover the plant's leaves.

4. Set the plant in a sunny window.

5. Add a few drops of liquid fertilizer. Follow directions on the package for exact quantities.

6. Change the water if it becomes cloudy or smelly. Add more fertilizer each time you change the water.

WATER GARDEN PLANTS

Make a whole water garden. Think of other creative ways to decorate your jars. Try these houseplants that also grow well in water.

- *begonia*
- *Chinese evergreen*
- *coleus*
- *impatiens*
- *philodendron*
- *pothos*
- *spider plant*
- *wandering Jew*

Topsy-Turvy Tin Cans

Most of the time you plant your garden right side up. But these plants can grow upside down. If you're feeling really creative, try making more than one.

What You'll Need

- empty metal coffee can with a snap-on plastic lid
- can opener
- pliers
- wire
- scissors
- masking tape
- coffee filter
- nail
- hammer
- colorful scrap of fabric
- glue
- houseplant such as a golden pothos or a heartleaf philodendron

MORE PLANT CHOICES 🌿

Many fruits and vegetables grow well upside down. Try planting peppers, tomatoes, or strawberries in your tin can. Flowers such as nasturtiums or petunias will work as well.

Instructions

1. If the can has a paper label, remove it. Soak can in hot water if the label won't easily come off. With a can opener, remove the bottom of the can. Be careful of sharp edges. Flatten any sharp edges with the pliers.

2. With a hammer and nail, have an adult help you punch two holes on opposite sides of the can, about 0.25 inch (6 mm) above the bottom rim.

3. Wrap the wire through the holes in the can to form a handle. Bend the wire upward. Twist the wire on each side of the hole to secure it in place.

4. Make a cut from the edge to the center of the coffee filter. Cut out a small circle in the center just big enough to fit around the stem of the plant.

5. Wrap the coffee filter around the plant near the roots. Place the roots inside the top of the can, with the coffee filter outside the can. Tape it in place with masking tape.

6. With an adult's help, cut a 2-inch (5-cm) hole out of the center of the plastic lid.

7. Hold the plant's leaves together and carefully feed them through the lid. Snap the lid on the can's top. Wrap tape around the edge to hold it in place.

8. Cut a rectangle of fabric 1 inch (2.5 cm) wider than the can and just long enough to wrap around it.

9. Spread glue over the back of the fabric and wrap it around the can. Fold the extra material over the bottom edge of the can. Smooth out any wrinkles and let it dry.

10. Hold the can with the plant hanging down, and fill in potting soil around the roots. Hang it from a hook or curtain rod. Water the soil through the top opening of the can whenever it feels dry.

Groovy Tie-Dye Garden

Grow your own natural dyes. Then use them to make a groovy tie-dyed T-shirt. Natural dyes are beautiful and friendly to the environment.

What You'll Need

- 2 x 2 foot (60 x 60 cm) garden bed
- garden stakes
- 1 packet red beet seeds
- 1 packet spinach seeds

Instructions

Plant your tie-dye garden in spring, when soil temperature is above 50 degrees Fahrenheit (10 degrees Celsius).

1. Prepare garden bed. Remove weeds and grass, and turn soil over with a spade. Rake it smooth.

2. Divide the plot into four sections. Mark the corners of each section with garden stakes.

3. Plant two squares of red beets, with nine seeds per square. Plant them 0.5 inch (1.3 cm) deep, spaced evenly throughout the square.

4. Plant spinach in the remaining two squares in the same way.

5. Weed and water your garden as needed.

6. Harvest beets when the beetroot begins to stick out of the soil. Let them get fairly large. Harvest spinach when leaves are large and fully formed. Snip them off at the stem.

Making Natural Dyes

Once you've harvested your veggies, you can create a one-of-a-kind T-shirt!

What You'll Need

- 2 white cotton T-shirts
- rubber bands
- 5 cups (680 grams) red beets
- 5 cups (150 grams) spinach
- cheesecloth
- 3 cups (710 mL) vinegar
- water
- 2 bowls
- 3 large pots
- wooden spoon
- tongs or similar kitchen utensil

Instructions

1. Chop spinach and red beets and place in separate bowls.

2. Place beets and 10 cups (2.4 liters) water in a large pot. Cover and bring to a boil.

3. Turn the heat down and simmer for about an hour, and then strain the liquid through a cheesecloth. Set liquid aside.

4. Repeat the steps 2 and 3 for the spinach.

5. While the beets and spinach are simmering, mix vinegar and 12 cups (2.8 l) water in a large pot.

6. Place the T-shirts in the vinegar and water mixture.

7. Bring the pot to a boil, then turn the heat to low and simmer for 1 hour.

8. Let the shirts cool down. Remove them from the water. Wring out excess moisture. Then twist sections of each shirt tightly. Wrap rubber bands around the sections as tightly as you can to hold them in place.

9. Place one T-shirt in each pot of dye. Use tongs or another kitchen utensil to make sure it is completely submerged.

10. Let the shirts simmer in the dye for 1 hour on low heat.

11. Turn the stove off. Leave the shirts in the dye for 12 to 24 more hours. The longer they soak, the brighter the color will be. The color will lighten as it dries.

12. Rinse each shirt well and hang to dry. The wet dye can stain other items, so be careful where you hang it.

13. Wait several days before washing the shirts to let the dye set. Hand wash in cold water.

Rainbow Herb Garden

Plant this handy herb garden in colorful containers. Hang from a post or fence for a cheery display.

What You'll Need

- 5 tin cans
- pliers
- 5 brightly colored outdoor or acrylic paints
- paintbrush
- nail
- hammer
- gravel
- potting soil
- 1.5 feet (45 cm) of wire
- nail or hook
- choose one of the following for each can: basil, oregano, thyme, sage, parsley, or cilantro seeds or plants

Instructions

1. Wash tin cans and remove labels. Soak cans in hot water if the label won't easily come off.

2. Carefully use the pliers to flatten any sharp edges around the rim of the cans.

3. Paint each can a different color. Let it dry for several hours

4. Give the cans a second coat of paint. Let dry overnight.

5. Have an adult help you punch three holes for drainage in the bottom of each can by hammering a nail into it. Punch another two holes 1 inch (2.5 cm) below the rim, on opposite sides of the can.

6. Place a layer of gravel in the bottom of each can. Add potting soil to within 1 inch (2.5 cm) of the rim or 3 inches (7.5 cm) if you are starting with plants instead of seeds.

7. Place plants in the pots and fill in soil around them to within 1 inch (2.5 cm) of the rim. Press firmly to hold them in place. If using seeds, sprinkle them over the surface of the soil. Cover with a thin layer of soil about 1/8 inch (3 mm) thick.

8. String wire through one of the holes near the rim. Twist the end up and around the wire to hold it in place. Put the other end of the wire through the opposite hole, and twist wire up and around to hold it in place. Repeat for each can.

9. Hang the cans from a nail or hook on a post or fence.

10. Water your herbs daily.

11. Harvest when the herbs are 4–6 inches (10–15 cm) tall and leafy. Snip stems with scissors so they will continue to grow.

INDOOR OPTION

If you don't have space outdoors, hang your cans indoors near a sunny window.

23

Pretty Pallet Garden

Turn an old pallet into a space-saving vertical garden. You can plant any small outdoor plant in a pallet. Try using plants that will attract butterflies or other wildlife.

What You'll Need

- 1 wooden pallet
- sandpaper
- hammer and nails
- 2 bags potting soil
- any combination of 4 (more for larger pallets) six-packs of colorful flowers, such as petunias, pansies, sweet alyssums, lantanas, and zinnias
- landscape fabric
- staple gun with staples

Instructions

1. Wash your pallet, and let it dry. Sand down rough edges. Have an adult help you nail down any loose boards.

2. Use a staple gun to attach a double layer of landscape fabric to the back, sides, and bottom of the pallet. Fold over each corner and staple down. Use plenty of staples to hold the fabric in place.

3. Lay pallet flat on the ground and pour potting soil over it. Push soil under each slat, or board across the front of the pallet, to fill the spaces.

4. Starting at the bottom of the pallet, plant six flowers in each row between the slats. For each plant, use your fingers to scoop a hole in the soil and set the roots inside. Press soil firmly around the roots. Then plant 6 plants across the top of the pallet in the same way. Add a little more soil, and press tightly around each plant to hold it firmly in place.

5. Water your plants daily. Leave the pallet flat on the ground in a sunny place for several weeks so the roots can grow.

6. Once the plants are well rooted, lean the pallet up against a wall or other upright surface.

PAINTED PALLET

Paint your pallet with outdoor paint before adding the landscape fabric and soil. Choose a cheery color to complement your flowers.

WHERE TO FIND PALLETS

Many stores discard pallets once they've unloaded them. Stop in and ask if you can have one. Look for a pallet that is in good shape, with no rotten or broken boards. If you choose to plant edible plants in the pallet, look for one that is heat treated instead of chemically treated. It should have the letters HT stamped on it.

Mosaic Block Garden

Paint a cinder block a bright, cheery color. Then create a mosaic. Add flowers or other plants to turn this boring brick into something beautiful

What You'll Need

- cinder block
- outdoor paint
- paintbrush
- pieces of broken pottery or mosaic tiles
- waterproof glue
- potting soil
- 2 plants of your choosing

Instructions

1. Paint the cinder block with outdoor paint. Let it dry for several hours. Add a second coat if needed. Let dry overnight.

2. Decorate the block with broken pottery pieces or mosaic tiles in a design of your choosing. Attach them with waterproof glue.

3. Set your block in a sunny spot. Fill the holes with potting soil to 3 inches (7.5 cm) below the top.

4. Set a plant in each hole. Fill in potting soil around them, and press firmly to hold them in place.

5. Water your plants daily.

CINDER BLOCK GARDEN

Decorate more blocks to create a whole cinder block garden. Set the blocks around the edge of a patio, or stack them in alternating directions. Mix in other flowers and foliage such as impatiens, petunias, pansies, or coleus.

Towering Trio

Stack three pots to create a colorful garden tower. Paint stripes, polka dots, or zigzags for extra pizzazz.

What You'll Need

- 1 small, 1 medium, and 1 large terra-cotta flowerpot
- 3 flower buckets, sized to fit upside down inside the flowerpots
- 3 or 4 different colors of outdoor paint
- paintbrush
- foam circle (or cut a new sponge into a circle)
- painter's tape
- potting soil
- 3 six-packs of mums
- ornamental grass

Instructions

1. Turn pots upside down and paint the outside of each. Let paint dry well. Add a second coat if needed.

2. Paint stripes, polka dots, or zigzags on the outside of each pot.

   - Mark the edges of each stripe or zigzag with painter's tape. Paint the area between the tape. Remove the tape after the paint dries.

   - Dip the foam circle in paint and press it on the pot to make polka dots.

3. Let the paint dry, then set an upside-down flower bucket inside each pot.

4. Fill in around the buckets with potting soil. Leave 3 inches (7.5 cm) space at the top.

5. Stack the pots on top of each other.

6. Plant flowers in the bottom two pots. Fill in around them with soil. Press firmly to hold the plants in place. Plant ornamental grass in top pot.

7. Set the pots in a sunny spot. Water them daily.

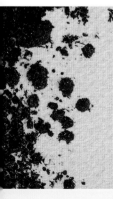

INDOOR OPTION

If you don't have space outdoors, plant a mini tower indoors. Use one 4-inch (10-cm) wide pot, one 6-inch (15-cm) wide pot, and an empty tin can. Decorate the pots as above. Then set the tin can upside down in the larger pot. Fill in around it with potting soil. Set the smaller pot on top and fill with potting soil. Plant small plants such as sweet alyssum or candytuft around the edge of the bottom pot and in the top pot.

Battling Bugs

There's a war going on in your garden! Insect pests, slugs, and other animals can damage your plants. But not all the critters in your garden are harmful. Some pollinate your plants and even eat pests. How can you get rid of the bad guys without harming the good ones?

Keep Out!

The best way to deter pests is to keep your plants healthy and strong. Remove weeds where pests can hide. Don't let the soil get too wet or dry. Certain plants, such as marigolds, nasturtiums, and many herbs, naturally repel pests. If you have trouble with rabbits or deer eating your plants, you may need a fence to keep them out.

Pest Patrol

If you find insect pests, snails, or slugs on your plants, the simplest way to kill them is to pick them off and drop them into soapy water. One good pest killer you can buy is called diatomaceous earth. Sprinkle it over and around the edges of your garden. The sharp little diatoms do not hurt people or plants, but are deadly to insects and slugs. Diatomaceous earth is sold at department stores and home improvement stores.

HARMFUL INVADERS

aphids

cabbage worms

corn earworms

cucumber beetles

flea beetles

Mexican bean beetles

potato beetles

slugs and snails

squash bug

tomato hornworms

HELPFUL VISITORS

earthworms

ground beetles

hover flies

lacewings

lady beetles

praying mantises

soldier beetles

spiders

tachinid flies

toads

SAFETY TIP

When using pesticides, be sure to follow the instructions on the package.

Read More

Brown, Renata Fossen. *Gardening Lab for Kids.* Hands-On Family. Beverly, Mass.: Quarry Books, 2014.

Cornell, Kari A. *The Nitty-Gritty Gardening Book: Fun Projects for All Seasons.* Minneapolis, Minn.: Millbrook Press, 2015.

Lay, Richard. *A Green Kid's Guide to Soil Preparation.* A Green Kid's Guide to Gardening! Minneapolis, Minn.: Magic Wagon, 2013.

Internet Sites

FactHound offers a safe, fun way to find Internet sites related to this book. All of the sites on FactHound have been researched by our staff.

Here's all you do:

Visit *www.facthound.com*

Type in this code: 9781491482377

Super-cool stuff! Check out projects, games and lots more at **www.capstonekids.com**

Books in this series: